Protecting Your Money When Purchasing or Remodeling a House

Practical Pointers From An Attorney

By: David Merbaum, Esq.

Merbaum Law Group P.C.

Dedication

To Michele

TABLE OF CONTENTS

CHAPTER 1   1
Introduction
CHAPTER 2   3
Remodeling
CHAPTER 3   17
New House Purchase
CHAPTER 4   21
New House Construction
CHAPTER 5   23
Purchasing a Re-Sale
CHAPTER 6   25
Inspections and Maintenance Tips
CHAPTER 7   29
Dispute Resolution
CHAPTER 8   33
Claims of Lien
CONCLUSION   35

FORMS   37
RESOURCES   45

DISCLAIMER

This book is not intended to provide legal advice, nor does it constitute the creation of an attorney client relationship. The forms provided herein are for informational purposes and should only be used after consultation with an experienced attorney. Each situation is different and the recommendations and advice contained herein may not be applicable to all persons or factual situations.

Chapter 1
Introduction

Why should I read this book?

As an attorney whose practice focuses on construction-related issues, I am frequently contacted by people from all walks of life who have run into problems relating to home remodeling or the purchase of a home.

I have heard all sorts of stories such as, "I gave the contractor money, and he didn't finish the job," "The contractor was highly recommended but his work was terrible," or, "I just moved into the house and discovered that there is water damage. Why didn't my inspector discover the leak, and why didn't the seller tell me that there was water damage?"

In each instance, something could have been done in advance to prevent the problem. As the old adage goes, an ounce of prevention is worth a pound of cure. In the following chapters, I will provide some practical pointers and advice that will help you protect yourself from losing your hard-earned money, whether you are simply remodeling your home, or you are buying a new home. Although the book refers to Georgia laws, the advice and recommendations are widely applicable.

Chapter 2
REMODELING

Trying not to make it a trying experience

Remodeling a house can be a trying experience. If the project includes the kitchen or the bathroom, it can be quite an inconvenience. Ask the contractor to give you an accurate schedule of the work, and then expect him or her to stick to the schedule. Any delays can quickly become an annoyance, as you may not have access to your kitchen or bathroom for an extended period. In addition, if you cannot access your kitchen, you may have to eat out for several weeks, which can become costly. If you are finishing the basement, and you typically use it to store household items, you may have to place those items in storage for months. Any delays by the contractor can cost you money. So how do you find a good contractor, and how can you make sure the job is done on time and done properly?

HOW TO FIND A QUALIFIED CONTRACTOR

Although it may seem obvious, the goal in selecting a contractor is to find one who is capable and qualified to do the work. How do you find a good contractor? It will take some time and effort in the beginning of the process, but this can save you a tremendous amount of money and headaches at the end. One way to find a contractor is to ask friends, neighbors, and relatives for a referral. I am certain that you know at least one friend or relative that has employed a contractor. Go to one of the do-it-yourself stores such as Lowe's or The Home Depot and ask some of the people who work there if they can recommend a contractor. Go to some of the stores where contractors purchase building materials such as Ferguson Enterprises, Inc., Progressive Lighting, Inc., Plumbing Distributors, Inc., or the lumberyard, and ask the guys behind the counter if they recommend someone in particular. This is the first step in finding a qualified contractor.

Once you have a few names, contact the Better Business Bureau (BBB), or go to its website to see if any complaints have been lodged against the contractor. The website will tell you the number of complaints filed against a contractor, if any, and whether they were resolved. I suggest you be wary if there have been lots of complaints, even if they all have been resolved. In my opinion, five to eight complaints over a three-year period constitutes too many. Most people do not immediately go to the BBB to file a complaint. They normally try to work things out, and even then, it takes some time and effort to register a complaint officially. So, even if all of the complaints have been resolved, the fact that there are so many complaints should be a concern, as you can assume that the contractor must have caused the customer a lot of trouble in order for the customer to feel compelled to make a complaint.

QUESTIONS, QUESTIONS, AND MORE QUESTIONS

Before you sign any agreements, it is vital that you determine whether you are dealing with an individual or a corporation. The way to do this is to go to the Corporations page of the Georgia Secretary of State website. If you are dealing with a Georgia corporation, you will find the date the business was incorporated as well as the names of the officers. Make sure you know the exact legal name of the business because if you do not input the name properly, you may not find the information you need. Sometimes the company was incorporated in another state and then it registers in Georgia with the Georgia Secretary of State. While that alone is not a big issue, I might want to ask the contractor why they incorporated in another state.

You can also type in the name of the person with whom you are dealing to see if he is an officer of the company. If a Bill Wilson from Acme Builders, Inc. says he runs the company, but you see that his wife is listed as the president and CEO and occupies all other positions in the company, you should be a little concerned.

Perhaps he put the company in his wife's name to protect himself from some claims. If you can search to see if "Bill Wilson" is an officer of any other entities, you should do that. If he is affiliated with other companies, ask him about those other entities and how they relate, if at all, to the one you will be dealing with. If several inactive or administratively dissolved companies are listed, you should be concerned. Sometimes when a company has judgments against it or is in financial trouble, the owners simply let it die and start a new corporation. Look to see when the company was first incorporated. If it was recently incorporated, and Bill tells you he has been involved with the company for ten years, you will want to ask Bill why the company is only a few months old. You can also call the Secretary of State and ask questions if you encounter any difficulties using their website. You may also want to ask the contractor if he or any of his companies have ever filed for bankruptcy.

Corporations are set up to avoid personal liability, as well as for other reasons. There is nothing wrong in dealing with a corporation. However, if you are dealing with one, you need to keep in mind that if you have to file a lawsuit, you can usually only proceed against the corporation and not the individuals you have dealt with.

It can be more difficult to collect a judgment against a corporation as opposed to an individual owner. You may also want to consider looking at court records to see if the contractor has been involved in litigation. When I was in court a few years ago, I met a woman who had sued a contractor for fifteen thousand dollars ($15,000). She said that she had paid the contractor, yet some of the work was incomplete, and the work that had been completed had not been done properly. The judge told her that she was about the tenth person to sue the builder in the past few years. The likelihood that the woman would ever see her money again was slim.

You can check the court records by going to the clerk of court (either in person or online) in the county where the contractor lives, if he is an individual, or where the corporation maintains its registered agent. The information of the registered agent can be found at the Secretary of State webpage discussed above. You will have to check state, superior, and magistrate court records if you want to cover all your bases. Some courts have computer databases in which you can search for any legal cases the company or individual has been involved in. You can ask the contractor if he or his company have ever been involved in a lawsuit or an arbitration proceeding resulting from a job, but you may not receive an honest answer.

You can also do an Internet search on a contractor and see what shows up. In today's world, information about a disreputable company spreads quickly, and it is easy to find what you need online. Other sources include Angie's List and kudzu.com. You might have publications delivered to your home that claim to offer a listing of contractors who have been rated positively and are reputable companies to deal with. Many companies pay to be included in these types of publications. That is not to say that these are not reputable and reliable businesses; it's just that the mere inclusion in such publications does not ensure that they are top-notch businesses.

Once you have the names of a few contractors and have done some research on them, schedule appointments to meet each one so that you can get estimates of the work you want done. If you schedule an appointment for an estimate and the contractor is late, that is not a good sign. If the contractor cannot show up for an appointment before he has your money, why would he show up after he has your money? Certainly, there are reasons that people are late for appointments. However, the fact that the contractor is late for the first meeting should be one factor to consider when making a final decision.

Follow the contractor around as he does the estimate. Compare all the estimates you receive from the contractors you've chosen, and examine the details carefully. You have to compare apples to apples. Ask for the job price per square foot. If an estimate is significantly more or less than the others, find out why. Did that contractor miss something, or is his low price simply a good deal? Many contractors give a low price in order to win a job, and then they demand changes once the work starts. If the price seems too good to be true, it probably is.

Don't only ask for a list of referrals; instead, ask for a list of the last three to five jobs that the contractor has completed. Consider that the contractor is only going to provide you with the names of satisfied customers as referrals. If there is a gap in the dates for the last three to five jobs, ask why there is a gap. He may not want to tell you about a certain job, or he may not have had any work during that time, both of which may be of concern.

Ask the contractor if he has performed this type of work before. Perhaps you are doing a kitchen renovation. This usually involves removal and replacement of counters and appliances, and the placement of new or re-routed plumbing and related electrical work. The contractor may have remodeling experience, but perhaps he usually remodels basements or only performs exterior work. Simply stated, make sure that the contractor can do the job that he says he can do.

Ask the contractor for the average dollar amount of his last few projects. You do not want yours to be the biggest job he has ever performed, as he may not be capable of handling a large job.

Ask the contractor how much of the work he will do himself or with his own crew as opposed to using subcontractors. You will want to know who will be on site to supervise the project for the contractor. Make sure that the person on site speaks your language as well.

Try to secure at least three bids that relate to the same scope of work. Make sure you are comparing apples to apples. Try to secure a fixed price that covers all of the work. While it is possible that contingencies might arise during the course of the work, you do not want to be on the hook for extensive changes once the contractor is well into the job. Sometimes a contractor simply gives you an allowance for a portion of the work. You typically see this for installation work, such as for carpeting, flooring, and cabinets, and even with painting jobs. An allowance is a certain dollar amount that is a part of the contract for a specific area of work. For example, you might have set an allowance of fifteen hundred dollars ($1,500) for carpet. You need to find out what kind of carpet you can get for that amount, and whether the padding and installation will be included as well. One contractor may give you a flat fee for carpet, and the other may give you an allowance. The bottom line is that you need to know the price per square foot for the carpet so you can compare the flat fee to the allowance. Using the flat fee may only get you a nine-dollar–per-square foot carpet while the other contractor may have included carpet valued at eighteen dollars per square foot. Normally, the more expensive the carpet is per square foot, the better the quality. The same analysis holds true for cabinets, lighting, and any other kind of work that is covered by an allowance.

GET A WRITTEN CONTRACT

Once you have researched the contractor and made a decision on whom to hire, make sure you receive a written contract. Ask the contractor if he has a form for a contract, or have an attorney prepare one for you. Do not proceed without a written contract that spells out in detail the work to be done, the amount to be paid, and the schedule for the work. Make sure you include the date by which the project will be completed. A few dollars spent up front with an attorney will protect you if there is a problem later on. Other important provisions include terms of payment, dispute resolution procedures, default procedures, and change order procedures. Georgia law requires the inclusion of certain language relating to dispute resolution in all contracts for residential work. This is discussed more fully in the Chapter 7. If you have issues along the way, I cannot stress enough that you should document the issues in writing. If the contractor fails to show up one day, send an e mail. If you have an issue with an invoice, don't wait a few weeks to complain. Send a letter, e mail or text message. Don't pay a bill that you have an issue with thinking that you will simply address it at the end. While you certainly do not want to anticipate that you will have issues, you have to protect yourself and document the issues as they happen in the event you end up on court later on. You may also want to include a provision that obligates the contractor to continue to work, even if there is a dispute, so this way you know that a dispute will not disrupt the project.

Many clients who come in to see me have paid the contractor a good chunk of money up front. I strongly discourage people from doing this. You are giving a total stranger your hard-earned money before he ever does a stitch of work at your home. Contractors will tell you they need the money to buy the materials. It is my opinion that if the contractor does not have enough money to buy materials to start a job, he is not an established contractor. You have no way to know whether he is taking your money to buy materials for another job. If you think you want to use the contractor, and he says he needs money for materials, ask for a list of materials and buy them yourself, and have them delivered to your house. You can also accompany the contractor to the store. He can pick out what is needed to start the job, and you can pay for it.

If the contractor fails to complete the project or never starts, you can make the materials available to the next contractor you hire, or you can return the materials to the store. Keep in mind, however, that there might be a restocking fee, but that is worth the cost as opposed to taking a chance that the contractor will take off with your money. The contractor is protected if you do not pay him, as he can file a claim of lien against your property. He knows where you live and how to find you. If the contractor takes off with *your* money, however, you may have to track him down, and may never see him or your money again. You have the most to lose, not the contractor!

I prefer that payments be tied to the percentages or phases of completion of the work. How do you know if the work is complete? You can retain a consultant to assist you in reviewing the work if you are not comfortable doing it yourself. If you are comfortable reviewing the work, then base the payments on the work you find to be acceptable. However, make sure you are comfortable undertaking this task. One client related a situation where the contractor started the framing, ran some electrical wires and then installed some sheetrock. The payments were tied into phases of work. The contractor asked for payment through the sheetrock phase even though the electrical was not complete and the project was not ready for sheetrock. This was a trick by the contractor to get the homeowner to pay up to the sheetrock phase by installing a few pieces of sheetrock when the project was clearly not ready for it. Sometimes the work has to be reviewed by the county or city inspector. Toward those ends, make sure up front whether a permit is required for the project. Call the county—do not take the contractor's word for it. If a permit is required, the county will ask for inspections before the plumbing and electrical work is covered up. Many homeowners are persuaded by the contractor to avoid getting a permit. The contractor may tell you that it will delay the project and it's a hassle to get an inspector out to the project. It may be a hassle, but the permit and inspection process is for your benefit. In fact, I have seen situations where a homeowner that is selling a house is asked if any work was performed without a permit, when a permit was required. If you fail to obtain a required permit, it may also provide a defense on a homeowner's insurance policy if you suffer a loss that is caused by or related to the unpermitted work. You can tie these inspections to payments. By way of example, you can correlate the payment to the contractor based on the following phases: framing, plumbing and electrical rough-in (this is when the plumbing and electrical wires and pipes are installed underground or behind the sheetrock inside the framing), drywall, painting, flooring, cabinets, and punch list. The more milestones you have, the less you will pay out each time so that the contractor does not get ahead of you. You only want to pay for work that is completed. It is very important to make sure that the contractor has not been paid more than the value of the work in place. This is your leverage and protection and once you lose that protection, it is difficult to get it back.

Make a schedule of payments part of your contract, and stick to it. It is important to comply with all terms of the contract. If the contract says that change orders have to be in writing and approved in advance of the work, make sure it is done in that fashion. If the contract specifies that no money is to be paid until certain work is done, make sure you follow the contract. If you deviate from the specific provisions in the contract and you get into a dispute with the contractor, he may argue that you waived certain provisions of the contract, and you will not be able to rely on those provisions if you end up in litigation with the contractor.

A waiver is an intentional relinquishment of a known right, and the contractor may argue that you waived your right to insist on written change orders if you allowed extra work to be done without a written change order in advance of the work. The contractor may also argue that there was a mutual departure from the terms of the contract. If you pay money that is not due or allow or agree to changes that are not in writing, the contractor may argue later that both sides mutually departed from the written provisions the contract and you cannot now rely on those written provisions. The provisions in the contract that benefit you are worth their weight in gold. If you disregard them, you defeat the purpose of the written agreement.

In addition to paying the contractor, you need to make sure that the contractor is paying his subcontractors and suppliers. If they are not paid, they could file a claim of lien on your property, and you could end up paying twice for the same thing: once to the contractor and a second time to the subcontractor or supplier. How do you avoid this problem? First, ask the contractor for a list of subcontractors and suppliers and attach that list to your contract. In exchange for each payment, ask the contractor to secure a lien waiver from the subcontractor and supplier. If you have any questions about the authenticity of the signature on the release, call the subcontractor or supplier directly to confirm that the signature is genuine. Lien waiver forms are included at the end of this book. Use the Interim Waiver for all payments other than the final payment and use the Final Waiver for the final payment. Alternatively, you can pay the subcontractors and suppliers with joint checks. A joint check is one that is made out to both the contractor and the supplier or subcontractor. In order to be deposited or cashed both payees will have to sign off on the check. Having your contractor give you a lien waiver for the money you pay him does not protect you if he does not pay his subcontractors or suppliers. You want to get a lien waiver from both your contractor and each of his subcontractors and suppliers. If the contractor asks that a check be made out to a different entity than the one on the contract or that the check be made out to his wife—this should raise a red flag. In addition to a Final Lien Waiver, you should obtain a Contractor's Affidavit at or around the time you make the final payment to the contractor for the remodeling work. Upon completion of the project or construction of your home, ask the contractor to execute an affidavit stating that the agreed price or reasonable value of the labor, service or materials has been paid or waived by the contractor. A form for this affidavit is contained at the back of the book. This affidavit, if proper in form and timing, can protect you from liens filed by subcontractors and suppliers after the execution of the affidavit. This affidavit, even if it is false, may protect you from liens that are filed subsequent to the execution of the Contractor's Affidavit. Any liens that were filed prior to the execution of the Contractor's Affidavit will not be affected. (Of course, if there are liens that are filed before final payment, you would certainly demand that the contractor have them removed before you make the final payment). A Contractor's Affidavit can dissolve subsequently filed liens if the affidavit is given as part of a transaction involving a loan in which the real estate is security for the repayment of the loan, involving conveyance of title in a bona fide sale or where final disbursement of the contract price is paid by the owner to the contractor at the time of settlement of the transaction. Therefore, as you can see, the Contractor's Affidavit is applicable in more than one situation. You must obtain the Contractor's Affidavit from the contractor, not a subcontractor. The Contractor's Affidavit must be a single affidavit and it must be sworn to as well.

For some reason, many people contact me for legal advice concerning problems they're having with landscapers. Contracting for landscape work is no different from contracting for interior work. Do not give the landscaper any money in advance unless you are absolutely certain you can trust the landscaper. Not all landscapers are capable of the same scope of work. Many landscape companies install grass and trees. Others also build retaining wall and walkways. Not every landscaper performs all of these services. Make sure the landscaper that you chose is well qualified to do the work that you are paying for. Many times, the problems with land-scaping work do not appear until several months after the work has been completed. Either the water does not drain properly, or the trees or sod dies. You have to make sure you are dealing with a business that has been around for some time. When the job is done, the landscaper will want to be paid in full, which is only fair. However, you will not know if the sod dies or the water pools up in the yard until several months later. You need to know that the landscaper will come back at that time despite the fact that he has been paid in full. Hiring a contractor or landscaper who has been in business locally for a fair amount of time makes it more likely that he will be around to address your warranty issues. Consider making the final payment with a credit card so in the event issues arise within your dispute period, you can exercise those rights with the credit card company.

ROOFERS AND HAIL DAMAGE

It seems that everyone in Atlanta thinks they have had hail damage. Almost every other week I receive an advertisement in my mailbox from a roofer telling me that I have hail damage. This is a sure-fire way to convince people they need a new roof when they don't. If you suspect that you have hail damage, make a claim on your insurance. Then follow all of the advice in this book to find a good, qualified, and honest roofer. Roofers are notorious for trolling neighborhoods and then convincing homeowners that they need a new roof. This is especially true after a severe storm. They will promise to contact your insurance company and convince the claims adjuster that you need a new roof. Moreover, after getting the insurance company to give you a new roof, the roofer tells you that they will do the work for the exact amount that your insurance company agreed to pay.

According to recent Georgia legislation, if you have entered into a written contract with a roofing contractor who is going to provide goods or services to be paid from the proceeds of a property and casualty insurance policy, you may cancel the contract prior to midnight on the fifth business day after you have received written notice from the insurer that all or any part of the claim or contract is not a covered loss under your policy. The notice must be in writing and sent to the contractor's address notated in the contract. Notice of cancellation, if given by mail, is effective upon deposit into the US mail with postage prepaid and addressed to the roofing contractor. In addition, before entering into a contract for the roofer to be paid for goods or services from the proceeds of a property and casualty insurance policy, the contractor shall do the following:

Furnish the insured a statement in boldface type a minimum of ten-point size font substantially as follows: You may cancel this contract at any time before midnight on the fifth business day after you have received written notification from your insurer that all or any part of the claim or contract is not a covered loss under the insurance policy. The right to cancel is in addition to any other rights of cancellation which may be found in state or federal law or regulation. See attached notice of cancellation form for an explanation of this right; and furnish each insured a fully completed form in duplicate, captioned "NOTICE OF CANCELLATION" which shall be attached to the contract but easily detachable and which shall contain in boldface type a minimum of ten points the following statement:

"NOTICE OF CANCELLATION"

If you are notified by your insurer that all or any part of the claim or contract is not a covered loss under the insurance policy, you may cancel the contract by mailing or delivering a signed and dated copy of this cancellation notice or any other written notice to (name of contractor) at (address of contractor's place of business) at any time prior to midnight on the fifth business day after you have received such notice from your insurer.

I HEREBY CANCEL THIS TRANSACTION
(Date)
(Insured's signature)

In addition, the new law provides that payment from the proceeds of a property and casualty insurance policy shall not be required from an insured until the five-day cancellation period has expired. (This provision will not relate to emergency services.)

Finally, a residential roofing contractor shall not represent or negotiate or offer or advertise to represent or negotiate on behalf of an owner or possessor of residential real estate on any insurance claim in connection with the repair or replacement of roof systems.

In addition to making sure that the roofing contractor complies with the law, make certain that your new roof is in compliance with your subdivision rules and regulations. Some subdivisions require you to install a higher quality of roofing shingles than the contractor might want to install (to cut his costs), and some homeowners' associations restrict the color or appearance the roof must have. You should make sure about all of this before hiring anyone to do any work. You may also need permission from your subdivision before undertaking this work. And as an aside, your subdivision may require permission for other type of improvements such as fences, new doors, significant landscaping or backyard sheds or play structures or even removing trees. Make sure the work is approved in advance so you do not get fined by your homeowners association!

Chapter 3
NEW HOME PURCHASE

Things are not always as they appear

You would be surprised at the number of clients who come in to see me about problems with new houses. Most people think that newer is better. Don't get me wrong—I understand the appeal of a new house. However, just because a house is new does not mean that it will be problem free. When you see a new house, you see fresh paint, new appliances, modern amenities, and fresh carpet or new hardwoods. Many new houses now have upscale appliances, lush landscaping, granite counters, and large closets. What you do not see is the way the house was built. And what you do not know is whether there are hidden problems.

Initially, if you are going to buy a new house, try to buy into an established community or completed subdivision, or at least a subdivision where it appears that the houses are being completed at a swift pace. While it used to be rare for this to happen, the Great Recession has made it quite common for developers to run out of funds before completing a planned subdivision. Therefore, you do not want to buy the first house completed in a subdivision unless you see that others are under construction and progress is being made toward completion of the entire community. Otherwise, your neighbor might be a big pile of dirt for quite some time. Also, when you visit one of these communities, you may see drawings and three-dimensional images showing promised amenities such as a pool, jogging track, tennis courts, and so on. Unless you have a crystal ball, there is no way to predict whether these amenities will ever be built. The agent or builder is trying to sell a house, so you need to take these promises with a grain of salt.

Talk to other owners who have purchased homes from the builder. Ask them how the house has stood up. You need to find out as much as you can about the builder. Most importantly, how has the builder responded to warranty claims or any other problems with the house? Did the builder come right out to fix the problem, or did he ignore or refuse to address the issue?

If the house has been on the market for a while, ask the selling agent about comments that other potential purchasers have made. They may have had concerns about things that you have not considered. Ask the agent if the builder has received any other offers on the house, and if so, inquire as to why those deals did not close. Did others find the house too small? Is the lot level? How does the house compare to other houses in the subdivision? Other than a slow market, there are usually reasons that a house has been sitting for some time, and you have to find out why.

If you conclude that the issues that other people have had with the house will not pose a problem for you, then you can take steps to purchase the house. However, remember that one day you may want to sell the house, and you will have to deal with all of those concerns again. What is right for you may not be right for someone else, so be prepared to deal with those issues when you sell the house. You may be able to overlook the steep driveway because you love everything else about the house, but when it is time to sell, you may have eliminated 50 percent of your potential purchasers.

If the house is vacant, visit it in different weather conditions. Try to visit the house when it is raining. This will allow you to see if there are any roof leaks or drainage problems. Walk around the house and look at the ceilings for any signs of moisture. Go into the attic and into the basement and take a close look for signs of water, or other damage. Walk around the perimeter of the house to see if water flows away from the house properly. Does the basement smell musty?

Examine the basement walls for signs of cracks. Although some settlement is normal, significant cracks could be a sign of a problem. Look for abnormally large or multiple cracks in the basement slab. Again, these could be signs of a problem. Inspect the driveway for cracks as well. Walk on the grass to see if there are any soft spots or lots of hills and valleys. Although rare, there may be a trash pit in the yard. Open and close the doors to the rooms. The doors should not swing open or close on their own. Open all the windows to see if they function properly. Don't just open one or two windows and assume they all work. Look for moisture between the panes of double pane windows. This usually indicates a blown seal and the entire window may have to be replaced.

If the basement is not finished, you can observe the workmanship of the builder in detail. Inspect the framing materials that were used to construct the home. Are there lots of knots in the wood? Did the contractor take the time to throw out the wood that was not in good condition? Look at the ductwork in the basement. Did the contractor take the time to direct the ducts neatly along the basement ceiling, or did he cut corners to save time and money? If you want to finish the basement at a later date, you may have to re-route all of the ductwork.

See how all of the wires and ducts are run in the attic, as well. Examine the furnace and air conditioning units to see if they are level. Make sure they are large enough to handle the size of the house (a qualified air conditioning company can assist you with this).

You also need to examine the property lines and determine what surrounds the lot. Is there a vacant piece of property that could be developed at some point in the future, which means all of those nice trees behind your property will be cut down? Can power lines be seen from the deck? Are you near a road that will create traffic noise? Will that nice two-lane road the house sits on be widened in a year or two? You must not only examine the house and the lot, but the surrounding environment as well. Are there horses or other livestock in the area that could attract rats or mice? Do the neighbors have dogs that bark all day and night? Of course, you need to check out the school system and make sure it meets your criteria as well.

Although it might seem that you have found your perfect dream house and you never intend to move, you must consider what will happen when you eventually try to sell the house. It is very easy to convince yourself that you can live with certain issues because you never plan to move. Some issues must be addressed, however; these are nearby power lines, houses with small or impractical backyards, houses with funky or uneven layouts, and lots that are not flat. You may like to be the house on the hill, but when you try to sell that house, you will find that most people are looking for flat lots.

Most importantly, after you have found your new home, hire an inspector to look at the house. I will address the issue of house inspectors in more detail in a later chapter, but the point I want to make here is that it is just as important to have a new house inspected as it is to have a re-sale house inspected.

CONTRACT REVIEW

Before you sign a new purchase and sale agreement, have an attorney review the contract. A good real estate attorney will help you make sure that everything you want in the contract is actually in the contract and enforceable. Time after time, I have had clients come in and tell me that the builder made all sorts of promises and representations about the house that turned out not to be true. Of course, these representations were nowhere to be found in their contracts. Later, when you ask the builder if you have received the upgraded security system you paid for, he may tell you that it was never a part of the contract.

During the contract negotiation stage, you and your inspector should walk through the house and make a list of items that need to be fixed or changed. Before the closing, there is typically a walk-through to make sure that everything the builder agreed to do before closing has actually been done. Take the time to review the list and the work. If necessary, ask the inspector to walk the house with you to make sure the work was done properly.

THE CLOSING

Typically, the lender and the real estate agent will each have an attorney present at the closing, and many buyers think these attorneys will look out for their interests, too. While most of these attorneys do a great job of explaining all of the documents, they are not there to represent you, the buyer.

Chapter 4
NEW HOUSE CONSTRUCTION

For the brave at heart

Instead of purchasing a re-sale or a new house, some brave people choose to hire a builder to construct a house for them. I find that people who choose to build a house usually end up doing it more than once. Just like buying a tract house or a re-sale, there are pitfalls to watch out for. First and foremost, it is important to choose a builder who has experience in building the type of house you want to build.

If your house will cost over a million dollars, find a builder who builds million-dollar houses. You have to select a builder who is comfortable with and understands people who build expensive homes. More likely than not, people who build expensive homes are going to be very particular and detail oriented. They take their time making selections, and they tend to change their minds several times before being satisfied with the finished product. A builder who has built expensive homes will know this.

As I explained before, do not do anything until you have a written contract with the builder. This contract should describe in detail, as much as possible, exactly what you are getting for your money. Most contracts will provide for allowances, which are dollar amounts for certain items such as lighting, appliances, cabinets, and so on. However, you should secure a firm agreement in regards to most of the other work. A set of plans and specifications should detail what the house will look like when construction is complete, and how it will be built. The contract should state when the house will be completed. Most likely, there will be many changes along the way. It is very tempting to simply discuss the changes with the builder and forget about them. It is fine to talk to the builder, but make sure the contract stipulates whether there will be costs involved if you make changes. You can avoid a lot of grief later on if you take the time to pay attention to details while the house is being constructed.

An issue I encounter quite frequently with my clients comes into play with both new construction and remodeling projects. Usually the husband and wife are involved at the inception of the project. However, once the work starts, one of the spouses gets busy with other things, and the other spouse deals with the construction issues. This person agrees to changes or asks for upgrades without consulting his or her spouse. Several months later, the builder presents a new invoice that details all of the changes that the one spouse agreed to, but the other did not know about. The lesson is that both spouses should keep track of what is going on so that there are no surprises at any point in the building process.

The advice and recommendations regarding the use of written contracts, inspection of the work, payment terms and waivers and releases discussed in Chapter 2 are applicable when building a new house as well.

Chapter 5
PURCHASING A RE-SALE

Purchasing a pre-owned house raises concerns as well. The key to purchasing a re-sale house is to find as much information as you can on the house. Find out why the sellers are selling the house. Are they moving? Do they have to sell the house because they cannot afford it anymore? This information will assist you in making an offer, and it may shed some light on how they have treated the house. If there have been financial issues, you may be concerned that they did not maintain the house properly.

The sellers are required to complete a disclosure statement that provides information about the house. Make sure you receive this disclosure statement and review it carefully. Look at the date it was completed. Since it is usually completed when the house is first listed, make sure that the information is not out of date. Ask the seller to sign the disclosure statement again so that you know the information is up to date. The seller is obligated to update the information, but most sellers do not do so after the initial form is prepared. Make sure all of the questions on the disclosure statement have been answered. If there are explanations for some of the answers, review the answers, and make sure that you understand the information.

Hire an inspector to inspect the property thoroughly. Visit the house while it is raining. If it smells musty, then there is probably a moisture problem. Moisture problems can be very difficult to solve. Unless you know that any moisture problems have been resolved, I would find another house. Look for signs of neglect. If the house has not been painted, you can assume that very little maintenance has been done to the rest of the house. If the filter in the air conditioner is dirty, you may have to put in a new system in the near future. If there is a sign of a leak, you have no way of knowing how long the house has been leaking and what kind of damage the leak has caused. Look to see if things have been covered up. A fresh coat of paint can cover a lot of problems. Don't assume that just because the house was recently painted the sellers maintained the house properly. The seller's agent provided the sellers with a lot of tips on how to market the house for sale. Some of those tips are to paint the house, mow the lawn, shine the hardwoods and put things into storage. If you understand those tips then you can be on the lookout for issues when you inspect the house. You may see all this closet space because the sellers put half of their clothes in storage. See if the kitchen has a pantry and where it is located. You do not want to walk to the hallway each time you need a can from the pantry.

Chapter 6
INSPECTIONS AND MAINTENANCE TIPS

HOME INSPECTORS

There are a large number of home inspectors in Atlanta. You have to find an inspector who is thorough, but who will not destroy your deal. You want the inspector to point out all defects and issues with the house, but he has to tell you which issues are the most critical. No house is perfect, and most sellers will not agree to correct every little item that an inspector finds. If you go back to the seller with a ten-page list of defects when only three or four really need to be repaired, you may lose out on a very nice house. You should be aware that the inspection is not a guarantee. The inspector's contract with you may provide that if he misses something and you rely on his report, he will not be liable to you for anything more than a refund of the price of the inspection. Ask the inspector how long he has been in the business. Although your real estate agent may suggest a very good inspector, you should find your own. The inspector referred by the real estate agent may not want to do anything that will kill the deal and cost the real estate agent his or her commission. An independent inspector is your best bet. An inspector that has experience as a county inspector or a builder is preferable.

TERMITES

Termites are a major problem in Georgia. If you are moving to the South from the North, you may not think about termites. You may not know how to recognize termites or the damage they cause. It is imperative that as soon as you move in, you have a reputable pest control company cover the house for termite treatment and repairs. You need to attain a repair bond as opposed to a treatment bond.

You want the termite company to inspect the property on a regular basis, provide treatment as needed, and agree to fix any termite damage caused to the house. When you own a house, you have to be observant of the house at all times. I do not mean that you should inspect it daily, but you should look for things that can cause problems if not attended to. With regard to termites, if you see thin lines in the sheetrock, or you can see that the wood around the windows is soft and deteriorating, you may have active infestation. If you see what appear to be winged ants flying around in the springtime, your house might have termite issues. Call the termite company at once and get them out to inspect and treat the house.

OTHER MAINTENANCE CONCERNS

GUTTERS

Keep the gutters free of leaves. Leaves that clog the gutters will prevent the water from flowing to the downspouts, and as a result, the water may flow over the gutter. This can result in rotted fascia boards, or it can damage the area around the excess water flow.

ROTTING WOOD

Watch for rotting wood and repair as necessary. Windowsills are especially prone to rotting, and may need to be inspected and repaired every once in a while. Consider replacing rotted wood with synthetic wood.

DECK POSTS

Look at the posts holding the deck. Some older houses have wooden or metal posts that go directly into the ground. The posts might be rotten or rusted underneath. If you buy a new house, or you replace the posts on a deck, make sure the posts are above ground and sitting on concrete footers.

AIR CONDITIONING FILTERS

Change the air conditioning filters monthly, or purchase a longer-lasting filter. Clogged filters can cause the air conditioning system to work at less than capacity, and may cause it not to work at all. Hire a heating and air conditioning company to service the units two to three times a year. Consider replacing older thermostats with newer digital ones.

Chapter 7
DISPUTE RESOLUTION

As hard as we may try to avoid problems, some matters simply cannot be resolved by the parties themselves. Most contracts have a dispute resolution procedure that provides for arbitration or litigation. Whatever method of dispute resolution you choose or agree to, keep in mind that it is always better to resolve the dispute on your own if possible. Usually, you will not want a judge, jury, or an arbitrator to decide your case, because there are never any guarantees of a positive outcome. No lawyer can or should guarantee the outcome of a case. Make every sincere effort to resolve your dispute before litigation. It is better to give up two thousand dollars ($2,000) to settle a case than to spend five thousand dollars ($5,000) or more in attorney fees and lose your two thousand dollars. Remember, a good settlement is usually one where both sides end up unhappy.

Georgia law requires that:

Upon entering into a contract for sale, construction, or improvement of a dwelling, the contractor shall provide notice to the owner of the dwelling of the contractor's right to resolve alleged construction defects before a claimant may commence litigation against the contractor. Such notice shall be conspicuous and may be included as part of the contract.

The full text of this law is included at the end of this book and details the method by which disputes are resolved. If you cannot resolve your dispute, whether it arises out of the purchase and sale of a house, a disagreement with a contractor, real estate agent, seller of a house, or any other party discussed in this book, you should consult an attorney. You might have options in Georgia on how to proceed. You can file a complaint in magistrate court when the damages are less than fifteen thousand dollars ($15,000).

Some people refer to this as small claims court. This is a fast and effective method of dispute resolution.

The downside of filing suit in magistrate court is twofold: One, either side can file an appeal if they do not like the result of the trial, and two, there are no provisions for discovery in magistrate court. Discovery is the process that allows you to gather documents and ask questions of the other side before trial. Without the ability to use discovery, trials in magistrate court are often "trial by ambush." Cases seeking in excess of fifteen thousand dollars can be filed in either state or superior court, and you will likely need an attorney to assist you. Corporations, including limited liability companies, can be represented by non-lawyers in magistrate court, but a company or a limited liability company must be represented by an attorney in state or magistrate court.

Often times the contract will provide that the parties will resolve their dispute through arbitration as opposed to litigation. In addition, some contracts require that the parties participate in mediation before they can file a lawsuit or initiate an arbitration proceeding. The contract may also detail how and where the mediation or arbitration is conducted. Mediation is a process whereby the parties meet with a neutral third party who may or may not be an attorney. They discuss the dispute with the goal of reaching a settlement that is agreeable to both parties.

The mediator cannot impose an agreement on either party, as he or she is merely a facilitator toward a settlement. If you cannot reach an agreement, you will be free to proceed with the next effort to resolve your dispute, which may be either litigation or arbitration. If you do reach a settlement in mediation, be certain to obtain a written settlement agreement detailing what each party has agreed to do. Arbitration is a binding process whereby a third person decides your case. The arbitrator is typically an attorney. The case is very similar to a case in court, but the rules of evidence are more relaxed, the hearing is usually conducted in a conference room, and the case is scheduled based on input from both parties and the arbitrator.

The arbitration can be conducted by a private arbitrator or by a company that provides arbitration services with several arbitrators to choose from. There are wide differences in arbitration providers in the Atlanta area. Some charge up front filing and administrative fees as well as hourly fees for the arbitrator. Others simply charge by the hour for the arbitrator. You may have to pay an administrative fee of close to one thousand dollars ($1,000) in order to file your complaint with the arbitration company.

When you review your contract, make sure you fully understand how any dispute will be resolved. Many people think that arbitration is faster and cheaper, but that is not always the case. If a specific arbitration forum is pre-printed in the contract, make certain you understand exactly who the arbitrator is and the costs associated with arbitration proceedings. If you are not comfortable with that provision of the contract, cross it out and consult with an attorney for advice about local mediators and arbitrators. The bottom line is that mediation and arbitration clauses in contracts can make it very expensive just to get in the door to have your dispute resolved.

Chapter 8
CONSTRUCTON LIENS

A construction lien (also called a mechanics or materialmans lien) is a claim made against a property by a contractor or other professional who has supplied labor or materials for work on that property. It is accomplished by filing a claim of lien in the office of the clerk of court in the county where the real property is located. Because the law requires that a copy of the claim of lien be mailed to the owner of the property via certified, registered, or overnight mail, the owner is always notified that a claim of lien has been filed against his or her property. Recent changes to the lien laws in Georgia allow the owner to demand that the lien claimant take certain actions by certain deadlines in order to make the lien valid. If a claim of lien is filed against your property, it is best to seek the advice of an attorney who is well versed in this very complex area of the law.

This chapter is not intended as a discussion of lien rights or the lien laws in Georgia; it is provided to notify you of why you do not want a claim of lien filed against your property, and how best to prevent it from happening. It is important to realize that as a property owner, you can end up paying for goods or services twice. For example, if you hire a contractor to remodel your home and pay that contractor for the work, but he fails to pay his suppliers or subcontractors, and they file claims of lien on your property, you may end up paying the suppliers and subcontractors to have the liens removed. The fact that you paid the contractor once may not be a defense to the claims of lien.

As discussed earlier in this book, there are ways to avoid having liens filed against your property. The easiest way to avoid this is to make sure you obtain lien waivers from every subcontractor and supplier who will furnish labor or materials for your job. Do not pay your contractor until he gives you the lien waivers from each supplier and subcontractor who will provide labor or materials.

Keep in mind that if the lien claimant follows the law and satisfies his obligations to file his lien, the lien will remain on the property until the claimant is paid. If you refinance or sell the property, you will have to deal with the lien. That typically means that you will have to pay it off, unless you find some legal defense to the claim of lien.

CONCLUSION

Buying a house, remodeling a house, or financing any other home project can be a very exciting process. Most people do not envision that things can go wrong. The contractor who comes to your home with all those beautiful pictures of other jobs he's done seems so nice and professional, and you want to trust him implicitly. The thought that this contractor might end up being the bane of your existence never crosses your mind. As an informed consumer, you must take steps to protect yourself. If you follow the advice detailed in this book, you will have a much better chance of avoiding problems, thus insuring the successful purchase or remodeling of your home.

FORMS

FINAL LIEN WAIVER
WAIVER AND RELEASE
UPON FINAL PAYMENT

STATE OF GEORGIA
COUNTY OF _____

The undersigned mechanic and/or materialman has been employed by _____(*FILL IN NAME OF PARTY THAT HIRED THE PERSON SIGNING THIS WAIVER*) to furnish _____(*DESCRIBE LABOR OR MATERIALS*) for the construction of improvements known as _____(*ADDRESS OF HOUSE WHERE WORK IS PERFORMED*), which is located in the City of _____, County of _____, and is owned by _____ (name of owner) and more particularly described as follows:

(DESCRIBE THE PROPERTY UPON WHICH THE IMPROVEMENTS WERE MADE BY USING EITHER A METES AND BOUNDS DESCRIPTION, THE LAND LOT DISTRICT, BLOCK AND LOT NUMBER, OR STREET ADDRESS OF THE PROJECT.)

Upon the receipt of the sum of $_____, the mechanic and/or materialman waives and releases any and all liens or claims of liens it has upon the foregoing described property or any rights against any labor and/or material bond on account of labor or materials, or both, furnished by the undersigned to or on account of said contractor for said property.

Given under hand and seal this _____ day of _____, 20___.

_____ (Seal)

_____

(Witness)

_____

(Address)

NOTICE: WHEN YOU EXECUTE AND SUBMIT THIS DOCU-
MENT, YOU SHALL BE CONCLUSIVELY DEEMED TO HAVE
BEEN PAID IN FULL THE AMOUNT STATED ABOVE, EVEN
IF YOU HAVE NOT ACTUALLY RECEIVED SUCH PAYMENT,
SIXTY DAYS AFTER THE DATE STATED ABOVE, UNLESS
YOU FILE EITHER AN AFFIDAVIT OF NONPAYMENT OR A
CLAIM OF LIEN PRIOR TO THE EXPIRATION OF SUCH SIX-
TY-DAY PERIOD. THE FAILURE TO INCLUDE THIS NOTICE
LANGUAGE ON THE FACE OF THE FORM SHALL RENDER
THE FORM UNENFORCEABLE AND INVALID AS A WAIVER
AND RELEASE UNDER O.C.G.A SECTION 44-14-366.

CONTRACTOR'S AFFIDAVIT

STATE OF GEORGIA

COUNTY OF _____

Personally appeared before me the undersigned attesting officer, duly authorized by law to administer oaths, the undersigned affiant, who after being duly sworn deposed and states as follows:

The statements made herein are on personal knowledge and relate to the property that is identified herein:

ADDRESS OF PROPERTY IMPROVED:

OWNER (S) OF IMPROVED PROPERTY

NAME OF CONTRACTOR

OFFICER OR MEMBER GIVING OATH

RELATIONSHIP OF PERSON GIVING OATH TO CONTRACTOR:

The above named contractor recently contracted with the above named property owner for certain construction and related improvements at the above described property.

The improvements have been fully completed pursuant to the terms of the contract or agreement between the Contractor and the Owners and any applicable changes, that the Contractor has paid in full the agreed price or reasonable value for all labor, materials, machinery, fixtures and services, including but not limited to services of architects, surveyors or engineers, furnished or performed by all persons or entities whatsoever in connection with or in relation to the improvement of the property. Moreover, there are no fixtures now installed in or on said property that have not been paid in full; that there are no contracts that are pending that have not been performed in full or terminated, that no disputes exist regarding any contracts made with respect to or in connection with the construction or repair of any improvements on said property with respect to the land itself.

Contractor further states under oath that there are no claims or rights to lien or any other claim for security for any obligation incurred for labor, materials or services provided in connection with the improvements of the property.

Contractor further states under oath that he is not aware nor has he received any Preliminary Notice of Lien Rights in connection with the property nor to his knowledge, has the owner of the property received any such notice except as follows:

The owner has paid contractor or for the account of the contractor in full, the agreed price or reasonable value of all labor, materials, fixtures, supplies, equipment and services including but not limited to the services of architects, laborers and engineers in connection with the construction or repair of improvements on the Property.

Affiant further states that this sworn statement is made to the Owner, purchaser or lender in conformance with O.C.G.A. 44-14-361.2 to induce _____(Owner, Purchaser or Lender) to purchase or make final disbursement or make a loan. Affiant states that he has personal knowledge of the matters stated herein and is fully authorized and qualified to make and give this affidavit on behalf of _____(Name of Company), that as _____(state office held) of _____(Name of Company) he is authorized by proper corporate resolutions to execute this affidavit.

_____
Individually
Sworn and subscribed to me
this __ day of _____, 20___

NOTARY PUBLIC
Signature and Seal

INTERIM WAIVER AND RELEASE UPON PAYMENT

STATE OF GEORGIA

COUNTY OF _____

    THE UNDERSIGNED MECHANIC AND/OR MATE-RIALMAN HAS BEEN EMPLOYED BY _____(*FILL IN NAME OF PARTY THAT HIRED THE PERSON SIGNING THIS WAIVER*) TO FURNISH _____ (*DESCRIBE MATERIALS AND/OR LABOR*) FOR THE CONSTRUCTION OF IMPROVE-MENTS KNOWN AS _____ (*ADDRESS OF HOUSE WHERE WORK IS PERFORMED*), WHICH IS LOCATED IN THE CITY OF_____, COUNTY OF _____, AND IS OWNED BY _____ (NAME OF OWNER) AND MORE PARTICULARLY DESCRIBED AS FOLLOWS:

(DESCRIBE THE PROPERTY UPON WHICH THE IMPROVE-MENTS WERE MADE BY USING EITHER A METES AND BOUNDS DESCRIPTION, THE LAND LOT DISTRICT, BLOCK AND LOT NUMBER, OR STREET ADDRESS OF THE PROJ-ECT.)

UPON THE RECEIPT OF THE SUM OF $_____, THE MECHANIC AND/OR MATERIALMAN WAIVES AND RELEASES ANY AND ALL LIENS OR CLAIMS OF LIENS IT HAS UPON THE FOREGOING DESCRIBED PROPERTY OR ANY RIGHTS AGAINST ANY LABOR AND/OR MATERIAL BOND THROUGH THE DATE OF _____ (DATE)

AND EXCEPTING THOSE RIGHTS AND LIENS THAT THE MECHANIC AND/OR MATERIALMAN MIGHT HAVE IN ANY RETAINED AMOUNTS, ON ACCOUNT OF LABOR OR MATERIALS, OR BOTH, FURNISHED BY THE UNDERSIGNED TO OR ON ACCOUNT OF SAID CONTRACTOR FOR SAID BUILDING OR PREMISES.

GIVEN UNDER HAND AND SEAL THIS _____

DAY OF_____, 20____.

_____ (SEAL)

_____

(WITNESS)

_____

(ADDRESS)

NOTICE: WHEN YOU EXECUTE AND SUBMIT THIS DOCUMENT, YOU SHALL BE CONCLUSIVELY DEEMED TO HAVE BEEN PAID IN FULL THE AMOUNT STATED ABOVE, EVEN IF YOU HAVE NOT ACTUALLY RECEIVED SUCH PAYMENT, SIXTY DAYS AFTER THE DATE STATED ABOVE UNLESS YOU FILE EITHER AN AFFIDAVIT OF NONPAYMENT OR A CLAIM OF LIEN PRIOR TO THE EXPIRATION OF SUCH SIXTY-DAY PERIOD. THE FAILURE TO INCLUDE THIS NOTICE LANGUAGE ON THE FACE OF THE FORM SHALL RENDER THE FORM UNENFORCEABLE AND INVALID AS A WAIVER AND RELEASE UNDER O.C.G.A 44-14-366.

CONTRACT PROVISION FOR RENOVATION WORK

§ 8-2-41. Notice to consumer prior to beginning initial construction work

(a) Upon entering into a contract for sale, construction, or improvement of a dwelling, the contractor shall provide notice to the owner of the dwelling of the contractor's right to resolve alleged construction defects before a claimant may commence litigation against the contractor. Such notice shall be conspicuous and may be included as part of the contract.

(b) The notice required by subsection (a) of this Code section shall be in substantially the following form:

GEORGIA LAW CONTAINS IMPORTANT REQUIREMENTS YOU MUST FOLLOW BEFORE YOU MAY FILE A LAWSUIT OR OTHER ACTION FOR DEFECTIVE CONSTRUCTION AGAINST THE CONTRACTOR WHO CONSTRUCTED, IMPROVED, OR REPAIRED YOUR HOME. NINETY DAYS BEFORE YOU FILE YOUR LAWSUIT OR OTHER ACTION, YOU MUST SERVE ON THE CONTRACTOR A WRITTEN NOTICE OF ANY CONSTRUCTION CONDITIONS YOU ALLEGE ARE DEFECTIVE. UNDER THE LAW, A CONTRACTOR HAS THE OPPORTUNITY TO MAKE AN OFFER TO REPAIR OR PAY FOR THE DEFECTS OR BOTH. YOU ARE NOT OBLIGATED TO ACCEPT ANY OFFER MADE BY A CONTRACTOR. THERE ARE STRICT

DEADLINES AND PROCEDURES UNDER STATE LAW, AND FAILURE TO FOLLOW THEM MAY AFFECT YOUR ABILITY TO FILE A LAWSUIT OR OTHER ACTION.

RESOURCES

http://www.sos.georgia.gov
google.com
kudzu.com
atlanta.bbb.org
O.C.G.A. 8-2-41
O.C.G.A. 8-3-331
O.C.G.A. 10-1-393
O.C.G.A. 8-2-40
Fulton County Courts
Superior:
    www.fcclk.org
State and Magistrate:
    www.georgiacourts.org//courts/fulton
Dekalb County Courts
    Superior: www.gsccca.org
    State and Magistrate: www.dekalbstatecourt.net
Gwinnett County Courts
    All Courts: www.gwinnettcourts.com
Cobb County Courts
    Superior: www.cobbsuperiorcourtclerk.com
    State: www.cobbstatecourtclerk.com
    Magistrate: www.magistrate.cobbcountyga.gov
Suggested Mediation Venues:
    JAMS: www.jamsadr.com
    George Reid: www.thereidfirm.com
    Miles Mediation: www.milesmediation.com
    Malow Mediation: www.malowmediation.com